Facts About Hummingbirds

A Picture Book for Kids

By Lisa Strattin

© 2013 Lisa Strattin

Revised © 2020

FREE BOOK

FOR ALL SUBSCRIBERS

LisaStrattin.com/Subscribe-Here

8 BOOK BOX SET

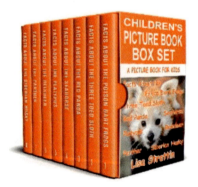

LisaStrattin.com/BookBundle

Facts for Kids Picture Books by Lisa Strattin

Pygmy Rabbit, Vol 153

Jumping Rabbit, Vol 154

Mini Rabbits, Vol 155

Blue Quail, Vol 156

Mountain Quail, Vol 157

Quokka, Vol 158

Quoll, Vol 159

Raccoon, Vol 160

Raccoon Dog, Vol 161

Radiated Tortoise, Vol 162

Sign Up for New Release Emails Here

http://LisaStrattin.com/subscribe-here

Contents

What Are Hummingbirds?

Hummingbirds: They are truly as sweet as their name sounds.

Hummingbirds are small, colorful birds with flickering feathers.

Where Did They Get Their Name?

Wondering from where did they get their name? Hummingbirds can flap their wings very fast, around 80 times per second. Do you know how long a second is? It's like the blink of an eye – and they are flapping their wings 80 times!

They make a humming sound when their wings flap so fast, this is where these little, sweet birds got their name. They can fly right, left, up and down, backwards, and even upside down, hovering by flapping their wings in an 8-pattern!!

How They Eat

Their long and narrowed bill is used for getting the nectar from long, tube-shaped flowers. Another interesting fact is that their feet are used only to rest on, not for walking or hopping.

Won't you love to know little more about this sweet, little bird?

Range

Typically, Hummingbirds are found only in Western Hemisphere, from south eastern Alaska to southern Chile. There are 320 different species of hummingbirds, of which 12 varieties spend their summer in North America and winter in the tropical regions.

Life Span

Hummingbirds usually have a longer lifespan, though it may vary from one species to another. The more popular North American varieties have an average lifespan of 3 to 5 years. In comparison to that, the smaller ones seldom live more than two years. However, broad-tailed hummingbirds have the record of at least 12 years of lifespan, while much larger Buff-belied hummingbird can live at least 11 years.

Diet

Hummingbirds generally feed on the nectar from flowers, insects, tree sap, and pollen. Due to their fast heartbeat, high body temperature, and breathing rate, they need to eat too often. They also need enormous amount of food every day to match their pace of activity. Hummingbirds have a long tongue to lick insects, nectar and pollen from flowers, and tree sap. They have the capability of 13 licks per second.

Behavior

Hummingbirds usually communicate through eyes. They display a typical defensive behavior, often, chasing away larger birds from their area. Don't go by their small size; they have the capability to chase away even hawks and other large birds.

Threats to Hummingbirds

Hummingbirds were killed in the past for their feathers, and till today, they face these threats. The destruction and loss of their habitat has proved fatal for their existence. These birds are adapted to a unique habitat, and hence, they have been listed as endangered or vulnerable species, now. Climate changes across the world are also affecting their pattern of migration, making it difficult for them to find food in different seasons.

As a ray of hope, many people are making the best attempt to create a natural habitat for hummingbirds in their garden, park, or backyard, with artificial feeders and flowers to provide them adequate food during the warmer months.

COLOR ME

COLOR ME

COLOR ME

COLOR ME

COLOR ME

COLOR ME

Please leave me a review here:

http://lisastrattin.com/Review-Vol-7

For more Kindle Downloads Visit Lisa Strattin Author Page on Amazon Author Central

http://amazon.com/author/lisastrattin

To see upcoming titles, visit my website at LisaStrattin.com– all books available on kindle!

http://lisastrattin.com

8 BOOK BOX SET

Facts About the Poison Dart Frogs

Facts About the Three Toed Sloth

Facts About the Red Panda

Facts About the Seahorse

Facts About the Platypus

Facts About the Reindeer

Facts About the Panther

Facts About the Siberian Husky

LisaStrattin.com/BookBundle

Stay Connected With Lisa

LisaStrattin.com/Facebook

LisaStrattin.com/Youtube

Made in the USA
Las Vegas, NV
27 June 2022